Reaching for

Meg Cichon García

Contents

A Harcourt Achieve Imprint

www.Rigby.com
1-800-531-5015

Chapter 1
An Incredible Task

Walking through a busy, crowded city, you are heading toward a place you've never been. All around you people hurry by, rushing in and out of buildings as buses and taxis speed down the street. It is a clear, sunny day, but you are shadowed by the enormous buildings that tower over you. You arch your neck back to take a closer look at these buildings and realize that they are so tall that you cannot even see the top of them.

In your hand, you hold a note.

Congratulations! You have just been voted Young Architect of the Year, and you have been selected to design a new building at the intersection of State Street and Independence Drive. The people who live and work in this neighborhood are depending on you to create the perfect building for this location. Your masterpiece must have the following features:

- It must be strong and safe.
- It must look good in its surroundings.
- It must meet the needs of this busy, crowded community, which is a place where people live, work, shop, dine, and play.

Ever since you got this letter in the mail, your mind has been filling up with great ideas. You picture a huge shopping mall, spread across miles of land. Sometimes you imagine a giant business center, where offices are surrounded by lakes and parks, and at other times, you dream of adding homes and apartments, soccer fields and basketball courts to this neighborhood. Maybe you can even combine those ideas into one amazing place that has it all.

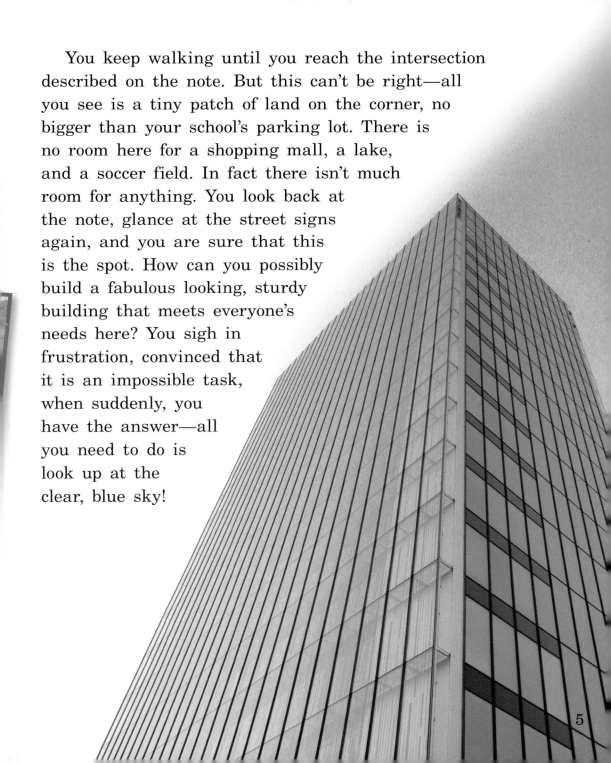

You keep walking until you reach the intersection described on the note. But this can't be right—all you see is a tiny patch of land on the corner, no bigger than your school's parking lot. There is no room here for a shopping mall, a lake, and a soccer field. In fact there isn't much room for anything. You look back at the note, glance at the street signs again, and you are sure that this is the spot. How can you possibly build a fabulous looking, sturdy building that meets everyone's needs here? You sigh in frustration, convinced that it is an impossible task, when suddenly, you have the answer—all you need to do is look up at the clear, blue sky!

Chapter 2
The Fight for Height

From the very first buildings to the skyscrapers of today, people have been trying to reach the sky and create incredible structures. You've heard of the pyramids of ancient Egypt, haven't you? Have you ever wondered how people long ago made the tallest towers? You've probably seen pictures of massive castles built hundreds of years ago. Taking a close look at these buildings will give you some ideas for your new building.

The Great Pyramid

The ancient Egyptian pyramids were very strong, and since that was a requirement for your building, too, maybe you should build a pyramid! The Egyptian pyramids were among the first very tall buildings, and are considered some of the most amazing structures of the ancient world. Built outside of Cairo, Egypt, the Great Pyramid was designed to be a tomb—or burial site—for King Khufu. It took more than 2 million stone blocks to build the Great Pyramid, which now stands about 450 feet high. But in order to support all those heavy blocks, the base of the pyramid had to be very wide. You don't have that much space, and a pyramid might not fit in very well with the rest of the buildings in this neighborhood.

From Bottom to Top

Have you ever used a deck of playing cards to build a pyramid of your own? You start by creating the layer on the bottom, and then you build a layer on top of that. But if you want to create a third layer, you have to make the base (the bottom layers) wider so they can support, or hold up, the layers on top. The same is true of buildings. For every layer that the building grows taller, more support must be added to the bottom to support the weight of the layers on top.

The Great Pyramid of Giza originally stood at 481 feet tall but lost about 30 feet as weather eroded the upper blocks.

The Great Pyramid			
Year built	Number of blocks	Weight of each block	Height
2600 B.C.	2.3 million	5000 pounds	450 feet

Two Types of Towers

Maybe you should consider building a simple tower instead—a tall and narrow tower would provide you with plenty of height and take up very little room on the ground. Many towers were built to protect castles and cities against enemies. Watching from the towers, soldiers could safely see when an enemy was coming because they were protected by the towers' high walls. The Tower of London is a group of towers that were built for this reason. Other towers, like Italy's Leaning Tower of Pisa, were designed as parts of churches.

The Tower of London was built to defend the city against enemies. Why might towers have been a good form of protection?

The people who built the Leaning Tower of Pisa expected it to stand 185 feet high, but they never achieved that goal. Unfortunately, the ground underneath the Leaning Tower of Pisa gradually began to sink during construction, and now the tower looks as though it might tip over. The trouble with many towers—not just the Leaning Tower of Pisa—is that they are made of very heavy stone, and putting holes in the stone walls for windows makes the walls weak. So if you wanted to build a stable tower, it couldn't have many windows, and it would be very dark inside the tower!

In 1990 the Leaning Tower of Pisa was closed for repairs. Engineers made the base of the tower more steady and straightened it about 15 inches to prevent it from falling.

A Source of Support

It sounds like your building is going to need more support than a tower could provide, and the builders of cathedrals (large churches) in Europe found a solution to this problem. Many cathedrals were built using long, stone arms called *flying buttresses* to support the cathedrals' weight. Made of brick or stone, flying buttresses were arched supports built along a building's outside walls to help hold them up. This allowed not only for height, but also for windows to be added without weakening the walls. The Notre Dame Cathedral in Paris, France, is 115 feet high and filled with colorful windows, thanks to the support of the many flying buttresses used.

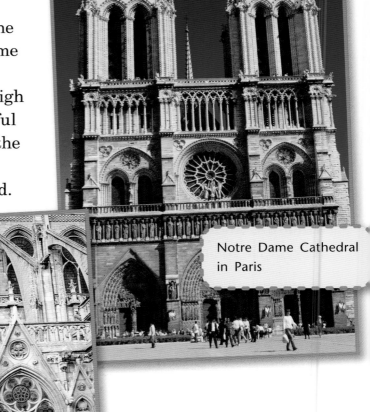

Notre Dame Cathedral in Paris

Flying buttresses

A Solution

A building with buttresses sounds sturdy and attractive, but a cathedral won't meet the needs of all the people who live in this community. While some people may work and worship there, it will not provide a place for people to live, shop, dine, or play.

In the 1800s builders in the United States faced a similar problem. The populations of cities like New York and Chicago were growing, but the cities were running out of land for new buildings. Architects and engineers, who are people who design buildings, had to figure out a way to build up instead of out. At that time it didn't make sense to construct, or build, a building that was more than four or five stories tall because people had to walk up all of those stairs. Fortunately, in 1857, the first passenger elevator was installed in a store in New York, suddenly making it more practical to construct taller buildings.

A Different Kind of Story

Story is another word for the levels, or floors, of a skyscraper. A ten-story building has ten levels or floors.

11

Now that elevators helped people easily get to the top of buildings, how could those buildings be designed so that they wouldn't collapse under their own weight? The answer came when engineers began to experiment with two lightweight metals, iron and steel, to create horizontal beams and vertical columns to support the buildings. Built in 1881 and standing ten stories tall, the Home Insurance Building in Chicago was the first structure to use this technology, and this building is considered by many to be the first skyscraper.

The Home Insurance Building in Chicago was one of the first tall buildings with many windows.

Graph It!

The **table** below shows the heights of some famous structures. A table is one way to display information, or **data**.

Building	Height (feet)
Great Pyramid, Cairo, Egypt	450
Leaning Tower of Pisa, Pisa, Italy	185
Notre Dame Cathedral, Paris, France	115
Home Insurance Building, Chicago, IL, U.S.A.	138

When data is grouped into the same category, such as height, you can use a **bar graph** to compare the data. The information from your table becomes the bars on your graph. You can see from the bars which building is the tallest.

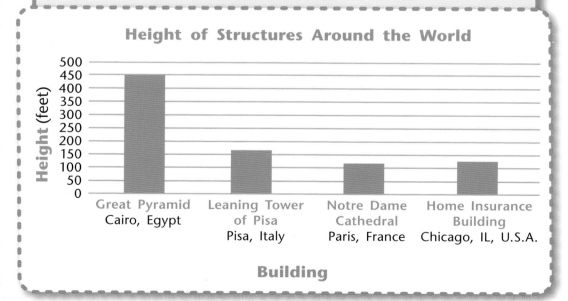

Chapter 3

It Starts at the Bottom

Building a skyscraper sounds like a good solution because a skyscraper will provide plenty of space through its height, withou taking up extra space on the ground—and without collapsing! So now that you know *what* you will do, the next question is *how?*

It takes more than a few beams and columns to build a skyscraper. Think back to the structure of the Great Pyramid; i order to support the weight of all those heavy blocks, the base o the pyramid had to be very wide. Skyscrapers are designed to b narrow, so how is all that weight supported?

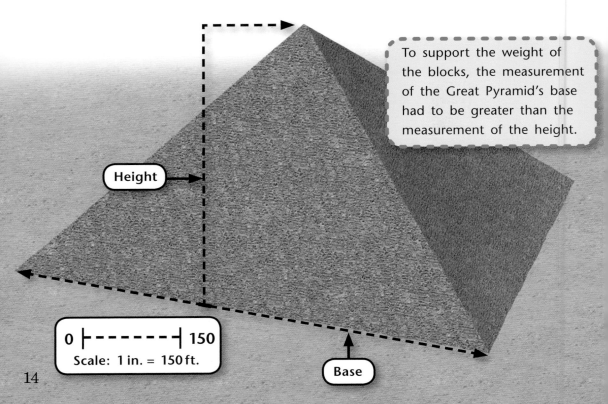

To support the weight of the blocks, the measurement of the Great Pyramid's base had to be greater than the measurement of the height.

Height

0 |– – – – – –| 150
Scale: 1 in. = 150 ft.

Base

Skyscrapers have two main parts—the part above the ground and the part below—and together, these two parts support the weight of the building. The part below the ground, or the foundation, usually consists of several layers of beams stacked on top of a thick layer of concrete. Above the ground, a steel frame made of beams and columns supports the building, just like your skeleton supports your body. The walls hang on the frame like curtains, but they don't hold up any of the building's weight. The beams and columns do all the work, supporting the weight of the walls, floors, and roof.

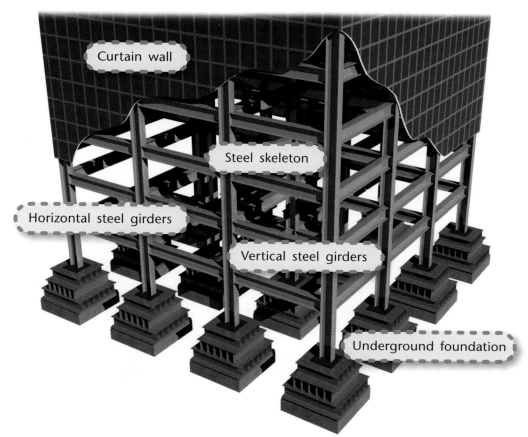

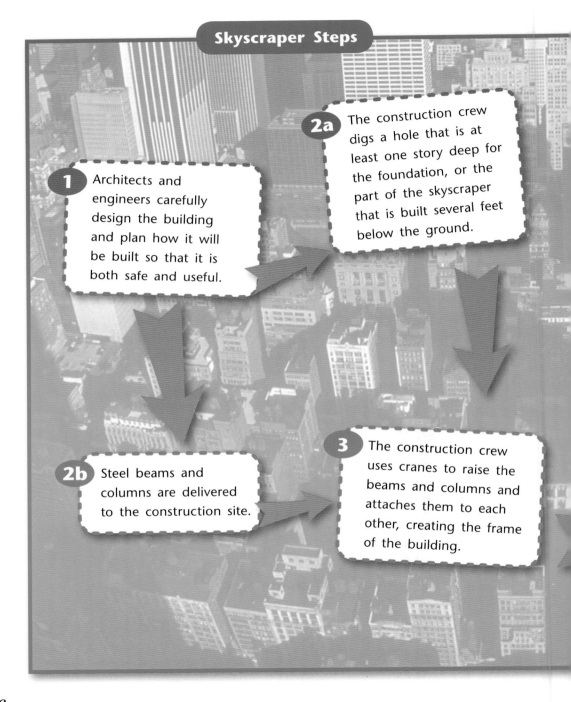

Skyscraper Steps

1 Architects and engineers carefully design the building and plan how it will be built so that it is both safe and useful.

2a The construction crew digs a hole that is at least one story deep for the foundation, or the part of the skyscraper that is built several feet below the ground.

2b Steel beams and columns are delivered to the construction site.

3 The construction crew uses cranes to raise the beams and columns and attaches them to each other, creating the frame of the building.

16

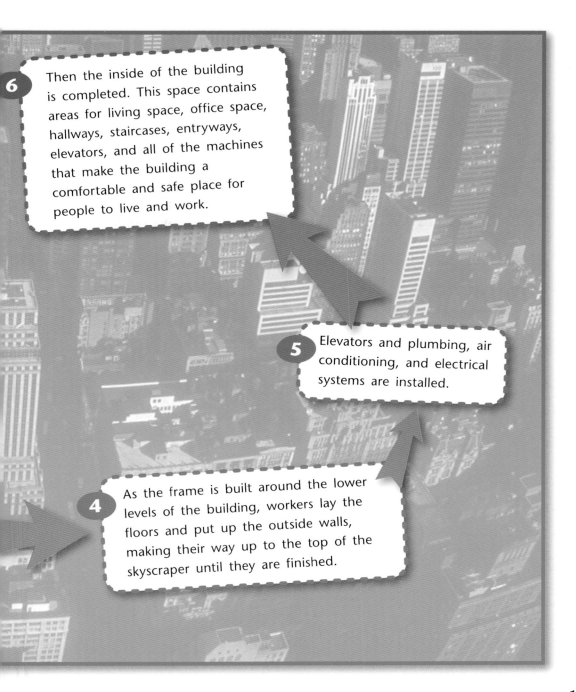

6 Then the inside of the building is completed. This space contains areas for living space, office space, hallways, staircases, entryways, elevators, and all of the machines that make the building a comfortable and safe place for people to live and work.

5 Elevators and plumbing, air conditioning, and electrical systems are installed.

4 As the frame is built around the lower levels of the building, workers lay the floors and put up the outside walls, making their way up to the top of the skyscraper until they are finished.

17

Graph It!

Have you thought about how much it is going to cost to build your skyscraper? Take a look at the data in this table to see just how the cost of construction has increased.

Building	Year Built	Cost
Chrysler Building, New York, NY, U.S.A.	1930	$20 million
Sears Tower, Chicago, IL, U.S.A.	1973	$150 million
Library Tower, Los Angeles, CA, U.S.A.	1990	$350 million

You can use a **line graph** to show how data has changed over time. If you plot the data from your table in a line graph, you can see that the price of building a skyscraper has risen sharply over time.

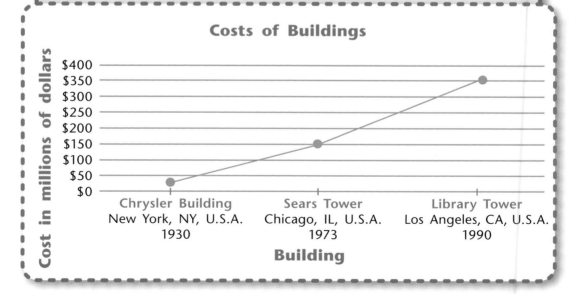

Chapter 4
Safety First

Now that you've figured out how to make your building comfortable and useful for the people who will live and work there, it's time to think about their safety. Because it is so tall, a skyscraper is a unique environment, and if there is an emergency, many of the people inside will be very far from a safe exit to the ground. As the person who is designing the building, you have a responsibility to be sure that the building is safe at all times: on windy days and stormy ones, and even during fires and earthquakes. The most important safety feature of a skyscraper is its structure, or the way that it is built.

Hundreds—maybe even thousands—of people will come to your skyscraper every day. Part of your job as the architect is to be sure that they will be safe while they are inside.

Wind

Skyscrapers are designed to sway with the wind so their structures do not bend from the wind's force. As the skyscraper is built, the columns and beams are attached tightly to each other on the tops, bottoms, and sides. This way when the wind blows, the whole structure moves as one piece, like a pole. If the columns and beams weren't attached, each section of the building would sway in several different directions, and the people inside would be very nervous!

Thunderstorm

Is it safe to be in a building that stands so close to the clouds? Many buildings, like New York City's Empire State Building, are safe in an ordinary thunderstorm with lightning rods—lightning strikes the rods, rather than the buildings, and the electric current from the lightning is safely sent to the ground through the skyscraper's construction. The Empire State Building is struck by lightning about 100 times per year!

The Empire State Building in New York City acts as a lightning rod.

Fire

Fires are especially dangerous in skyscrapers because hundreds of people in the building may be dozens of floors away from a safe exit. In order to protect people during a fire, most skyscrapers are supplied with complex sprinkler systems that put out most fires before they are able to spread very far, and many cities have guidelines about how emergency crews should respond to a fire in a skyscraper. The Petronas Towers in Malaysia are connected by a bridge on the forty-second floor so that in an emergency such as a fire, people can use the bridge as an escape route to move from one tower to the other.

Earthquake

Not only do you have to protect your building against wind, but you should also be prepared for an earthquake. During an earthquake large sections of the earth shift and break apart, causing the ground to shake. When the ground shakes, so do the buildings in the area where the earthquake occurs, damaging the buildings and sometimes even causing them to collapse. Many skyscrapers are designed so that the entire steel skeleton moves with the earth's vibrations during an earthquake. As the earth rocks from side to side, the entire building moves from side to side, too. This reduces the strain, or force and pressure, on the building, which keeps the building from falling apart.

21

Can you picture your skyscraper yet? You know that your building is going to be very tall, and you probably have some idea of what its frame will look like. But how will it look after all of the pieces have been put together? Part of your task is to create something that looks good!

The Home Insurance Building was one of the first tall buildings to include many windows in its design. People were not convinced that a tall building would remain standing, so they were wary about very tall buildings. Today designs focus on how the building will look as well as on how it will be built. Skyscraper design can include almost anything you can imagine.

New York City, 1880s

Skyscraper design has gone through many stages since the Home Insurance Building was created. Many architects and engineers have modeled their buildings after Classical Greek architecture, which included many tall columns in their design, while other buildings have featured extensive decorations. Walter Chrysler, the founder of the Chrysler Corporation, was in the automobile business. His Chrysler Building in New York City is decorated with hubcaps and hood ornaments, just like his famous cars.

The owner of the Chrysler Building had it decorated with items that would represent his automobile business. What would you like your skyscraper to represent?

As the construction of skyscrapers became easier and more popular and more of them were built in growing cities, all of these tall buildings began to block the light from the sun, and the cities began to grow dark. Eventually rules were established to prevent cities from falling in the shadows of miles and miles of tall buildings, which led to the creation of shorter skyscrapers that rise in height like steps. These rules also encouraged designers to include open areas called *plazas* with trees and parks around the bases of skyscrapers as well as shopping and entertainment on the ground levels so everyone could enjoy them.

Many skyscrapers have plazas like this one at the ground level. How might a plaza help a skyscraper fit in with the community?

Graph It!

How many stories will your building have? See how these skyscrapers measure up to each other.

Building	Year Built	Height in feet	Number of stories
Citicorp Center, New York, NY, U.S.A.	1977	915	59
Bank of China Tower, Hong Kong, China	1989	1,209	70
Taipei 101, Taipei, Taiwan	2004	1,670	101

Buildings have increased in height and in the number of stories they have. A **double-line graph** can show these two different sets of data on one graph.

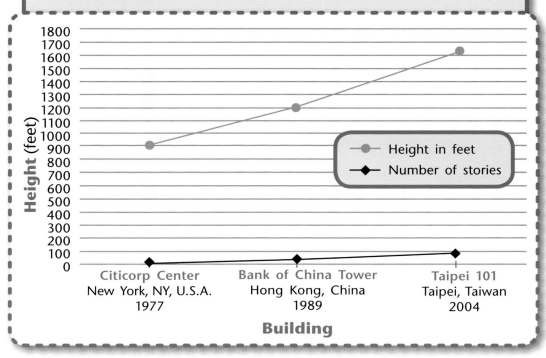

Chapter 6
What's Going On in There?

Your first responsibility in creating this building was to come up with a plan for a structure that would fit in the space you have, and then you had to figure out a way to make your building strong and safe. You know that a skyscraper can be built on a relatively small piece of land and still be both strong and safe. Now you have to think about how it will meet the needs of this community and provide a place where people can live, work, shop, dine, and play. Skyscrapers are so tall, and they hold so much space, so what goes on inside these super-structures?

From the outside, what goes on in these amazing buildings can seem like a mystery.

Skyscrapers of today serve many more purposes than they did when they were first built. At that time skyscrapers in the growing cities of Chicago and New York were originally designed as central locations where business could be done easily. Having offices, warehouses, and banks all in one central location meant that people could manage many tasks very efficiently because everything was in one place. It was not long, however, before people realized that skyscrapers could fulfill other needs as well.

Today skyscrapers provide space for more than just offices—now they contain apartments, stores, restaurants, hotels, health clubs, libraries, parking lots, and many other facilities. Chicago's John Hancock Center holds broadcasting facilities for radio and TV stations. The Petronas Towers in Malaysia have a symphony hall, a museum, and places of worship. New York City's Empire State Building even contains a movie theater that promises to make you feel like you're taking a tour of the city in a helicopter. Now it's up to you—what will your skyscraper include to meet the needs of this community?

Graph It!

Think about your skyscraper and how you would like to use all of its space. You have to determine how much space you will use for each area. These numbers can be expressed as percentages, but you have to be sure that they add up to 100%. Let's say that you've decided to divide the space in your building according to the data in the table below.

Apartments	Offices	Stores	Recreation	Parking
35%	30%	15%	15%	5%

You can use a **circle graph** to compare parts of something to the whole. Based on the data in your table, divide your circle to show how much space in your skyscraper will be allowed for each area.

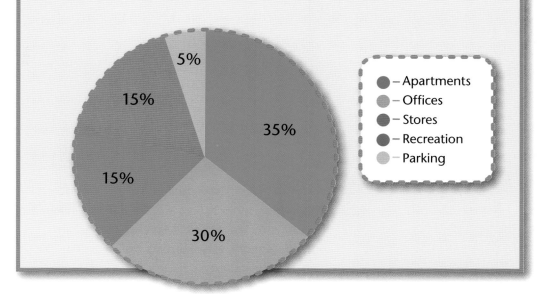

● – Apartments
● – Offices
● – Stores
● – Recreation
● – Parking

Chapter 7

The Tallest of the Tall

Do you want your skyscraper to be known around the world as one of the tallest structures ever built? For as long as people have been constructing buildings, they have been competing to create the tallest skyscraper in the world. Among architects and engineers, this is an exciting competition, and cities are proud to have the tallest skyscrapers in the world highlighting their skylines. However, this competition involves some disagreement about who the true winner really is.

While many of these buildings are considered skyscrapers, only a few are among the tallest buildings in the world. Many architects and engineers work very hard to build structures that are the tallest.

Graph It!

In the United States, height is usually measured in feet. In many other parts of the world, however, height is measured in meters. One meter is a little longer than three feet. You can compare the heights of some of the world's tallest buildings by creating a table.

Building	Height in feet	Height in meters
Taipei 101, Taipei, Taiwan	1670	509
Petronas Towers, Kuala Lumpur, Malaysia	1483	452
Sears Tower, Chicago, IL, U.S.A.	1450	442

When you want to compare two groups of data in similar categories, such as height in feet and meters, you can use a **double-bar graph**. The data becomes the bars on your graph; you can compare the information side by side.

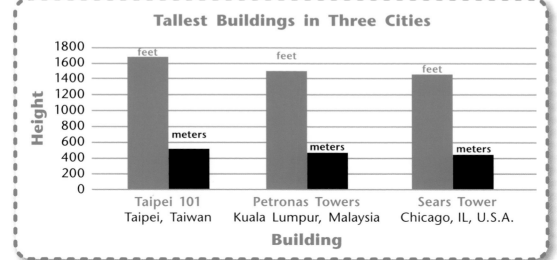

Tallest Buildings in Three Cities

31

Not everyone agrees on which structures should be included in the competition for the tallest skyscraper. Architects define a building as an enclosed space built to hold people. That leaves out many structures that do not hold people but are extremely tall, like Canada's CN Tower in Toronto, Ontario, which was built to provide special technology that would improve telephone reception. The CN Tower stands at 1,815 feet, making it taller than the world's tallest buildings, but if you want your building to enter the tallest skyscraper competition, remember to make room for people.

Although the CN Tower is taller than the tallest skyscrapers in the world, it is not considered the world's tallest building because it was not designed to hold many people.

The debate doesn't stop here. Some people who agree on this definition of a building have different opinions about who the current winner of the tallest building competition is. If rooftop antennas are included in the measurement, the Sears Tower in Chicago holds first prize at 1,707 feet. However, if antennas are not included, the height of the Sears Tower is 1,450 feet, and it loses the competition to the Petronas Towers in Malaysia. The Petronas Towers are topped by decorative spires, which *are* included in the measurement of their height, giving them a total of 1,483 feet.

Spire

Antenna

So which building really *is* the tallest? Spires do not contain floors, but according to architects, they are included in measurements of height, while antennas are not. Architects agree that spires should be included for one reason: they look good. Based on this ruling, the Petronas Towers are, in fact, taller that the Sears Tower. The Petronas Towers held the title of Tallest Building in the World for six years before being defeated by the Taipei 101. These three super-structures, the Taipei 101, the Petronas Towers, and the Sears Tower, are currently the three tallest buildings in the world.

Spires, such as the one on the Empire State Building, are architectural or decorative features that taper to a point and sit on top of skyscrapers. Spires are included in the height measurement of a building, but antennas are not.

Taipei 101

The Taipei 101 in Taipei, Taiwan was completed in 2004 and stands at 1,670 feet tall. Not only is it the tallest structure, but it also has the highest roof and the highest floor used by people. This super-structure contains stores, offices, restaurants, a fitness center, and the two fastest elevators in the world, with top speeds of over 55 feet in a single second.

Skyscraper Secrets

Each of the letters in the word *Taipei* stands for something the designers of this building hope it will represent.

Technology
Art
Innovation
People
Environment
Identity

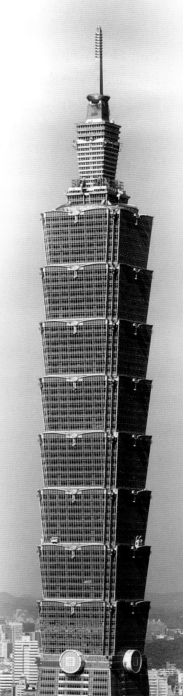

Petronas Towers

Each of the two Petronas Towers in Kuala Lumpur, Malaysia, stands at 1,483 feet tall, and together they are considered the second tallest building in the world. These two towers were built to hold Malaysia's petroleum company, Petronas, but they provide many other facilities as well. A skybridge on the 42nd floor connects the two identical towers, and the skybridge itself is two stories tall.

Skyscraper Secrets

The underground parking lot of the Petronas Towers can hold 4,500 cars.

All together the two Petronas Towers have 32,000 windows. Window washers spend an entire month washing the windows of each tower just once.

Sears Tower

Chicago's Sears Tower held the title of "tallest building in the world" for 22 years, with a height of 1,454 feet. Although the Petronas Towers are considered taller, the roof of the Sears Tower is higher than that of the Petronas Towers. Most of the Sears Tower consists of offices and some stores. On the 103rd floor, the Sears Tower has an observatory called the Skydeck, which is a place where visitors can look out the windows at the city below and see for miles in the distance.

Every year thousands of people take a peek at the sights of Chicago from the Skydeck on the 103rd floor of the Sears Tower.

Chapter 8
Towers of Tomorrow

So, have you decided what the future holds for your skyscraper? As far as some people are concerned, the sky is the limit when it comes to construction. Some engineers believe that it will be money, not technology, that will keep skyscrapers from getting much taller. Extremely tall buildings will require materials that are even stronger, bases that are even deeper, and specialized machines that will allow construction crews to lift materials and concrete up to the highest levels. Some people estimate that construction of these buildings could cost millions and millions of dollars.

Several experts think that the technology currently in use could support these super-structures. Others feel that lighter materials, faster elevators, and improvements in wind resistance will be needed. Still others believe that future technology could lead to the development of sky-high cities serving a million people or more.

Will your skyscraper serve the needs of this community here on the ground, or will it be part of a city in the clouds? Or do you just want to create the biggest and the best? Whatever you decide, you—and building designers just like you all over the world—can continue to reach for the sky.

Glossary

bar graph a type of graph used to compare data in the same category

circle graph a type of graph used to compare parts to a whole

data information, usually arranged in a table

double-bar graph a type of graph used to compare two groups of data in similar categories

double-line graph a type of line graph used to show the change in two different sets of data over time

line graph a type of graph usually used to show how data has changed over time

table a way of organizing data into rows and columns in order to display information

Index